Contents

LIBRARIES NI WITHDRAWN FROM STOCK

Introduction

London is the biggest city in Britain. Over seven million people live and work in London.

London is also one of the most important cities in the world. It is a centre for business and tourism.

There are many exciting things to do in London. The city has got some of the best theatres and museums in the world. There are a lot of places to go at night. It is a fun city!

This book begins with a brief history of London. Then we will look at things you can see and do in London today.

Shoppers in Oxford Street

1

History of London

The Romans

The Romans came to Britain in AD 43. They built a town on the River Thames. They called the town Londinium.

Soon, they built a bridge over the river. Londinium grew bigger. Ships came to the town from all over Europe.

The Romans built roads from Londinium to other parts of Britain. By the year 400, there were fifty thousand people living in the city.

Roman London was called Londinium

William the Conqueror

In 1066, William the Conqueror came to England. William was the Duke of Normandy in France. He won the Battle of Hastings and he became King of England.

William lived in London but he was afraid of the people of London. He built the White Tower to feel safe. Now it is the tallest part of the *Tower of London*.

Many tourists visit the Tower of London every year. *The Crown Jewels* – the Queen's gold and jewels – are kept there.

All the Kings and Queens of England lived in London. It was the biggest town in England. By 1600, there were more than two hundred thousand people living in London.

The Tower of London

Shakespeare's London

Shakespeare was born in Stratford-on-Avon in 1564. Later, he lived in London. Shakespeare wrote thirty-six plays. They are still read and performed all over the world.

The plays were performed in the *Globe Theatre*. The theatre was destroyed by a fire in 1613. In 1997, a new Globe Theatre was built in the same place. You can learn more about the new Globe Theatre in Chapter 5.

The new Globe Theatre

The Great Fire

The houses in Shakespeare's London were built very close to each other. They were made of wood. Sometimes there were small fires. On Saturday 2nd September 1666 there was a big fire.

It started in the house of the King's baker, in Pudding Lane, near London Bridge. Most of London burnt down. A quarter of a million people lost their homes. But only a few people died.

The Great Fire of London

Dickens' London

People built houses again after the Great Fire. But this time they built them of stone and brick. The city grew larger and larger. By 1830, there were more than one and a half million people in London.

The railways came and there were factories all over the city. The air was filled with smoke.

Many people were very poor and lived in terrible conditions. Most children did not go to school. Some of them worked all day in factories. Other children lived and died on the streets.

Charles Dickens lived from 1812 to 1870. He wrote about the lives of the rich and poor people of London at that time. He spent much of his life in London.

You can visit one of Dickens' homes in Doughty Street. There you can see his papers and writing desk.

London is very different today. You can learn more about modern London in Chapter 2.

London in Dickens' time

The River Thames

The River Thames is part of London's history. It has always been at the centre of the city.

Until 1749, there was only one bridge across the river: London Bridge. There were houses and shops on the bridge. Often, the river froze in the winter and people walked on the ice.

In the nineteenth century, many new bridges were built. Now there are more than twenty bridges over the River Thames. The *Millennium Bridge* and the *Hungerford* footbridges are new. Many of the Thames' bridges are lit up at night. They look very beautiful.

Tower Bridge at night

2
Places to Visit

You can visit many interesting places in London. You can find some of these places on the map on pages 14–15.

In London you are never far from the River Thames. Many tourists go on boat trips from *Tower Bridge* to *Westminster*.

Another good boat trip is to *Greenwich*. In Greenwich you can visit *The Old Royal Observatory*. The boat passes a lot of famous buildings.

A boat trip on the River Thames

There are some fine, modern buildings on the South Bank. You can see *The Royal Festival Hall* and *The Tate Modern*. There are also many art galleries, restaurants and bars on the South Bank.

On the South Bank, you can visit the *Imax Cinema* with its huge screen or you can go on the *London Eye*. The London Eye is a big wheel that takes you 135 metres above London. It is the slowest big wheel in the world and the best way to see the whole city. You can see for forty kilometres in all directions. You can see old buildings like *St Paul's Cathedral* and *Windsor Castle*, and new buildings like the *Millennium Dome* and the *Gherkin*.

The London Eye

The Gherkin is a glass building. It looks like a vegetable! From the London Eye you can also see the tall buildings in *Canary Wharf*. Canary Wharf is a new centre of business in London.

Most of the famous old buildings are north of the river. *The Houses of Parliament* are in Westminster. They are the centre of the British government. People call the tall clock tower by the Houses of Parliament *Big Ben*. In fact, Big Ben is the name of one of the bells. There are many government buildings in this area. *Downing Street* is nearby. The Prime Minister lives in number 10, Downing Street.

The Houses of Parliament

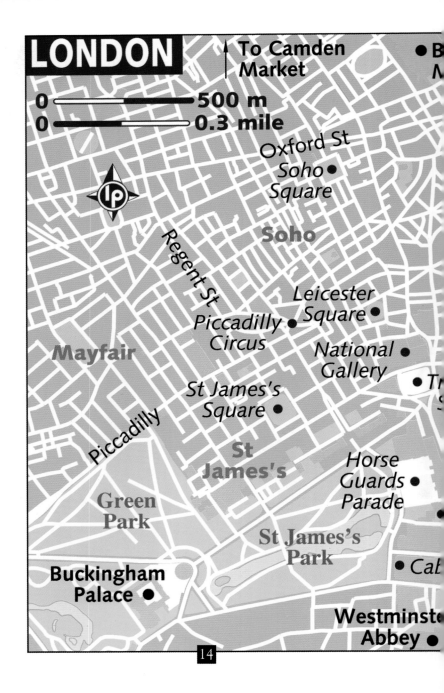

LONDON

To Camden
Market

● B
M

0 ══════════ 500 m
0 ══════════ 0.3 mile

Oxford St
Soho ●
Square

Soho

Regent St

Leicester
Square ●

Piccadilly
Circus ●

National ●
Gallery

● Tr
S

Mayfair

St James's
Square ●

Piccadilly

St
James's

Horse
Guards ●
Parade

Green
Park

St James's
Park

● Cal

Buckingham
Palace ●

Westminst
Abbey ●

14

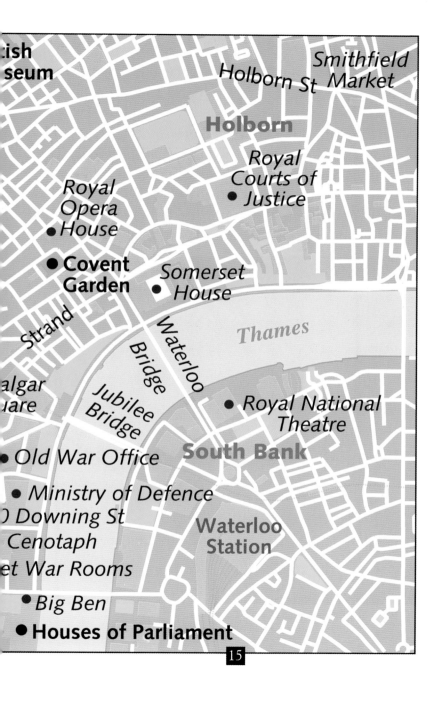

Churches

Westminster Abbey is one of the most famous churches in London. It is very near to the Houses of Parliament. The Abbey is more than nine hundred years old. In 1953, Queen Elizabeth II was crowned there.

Another great London church is *St Paul's Cathedral*. It was built by Sir Christopher Wren after the Great Fire of 1666. From the top there is a good view of the City of London. You can visit the cathedral by walking across The Millennium Bridge, from the South Bank.

The Millenium Bridge and St Paul's Cathedral

The National Gallery and the lions of Trafalgar Square

Art Galleries

You can find many art galleries in London. The most famous is the *National Gallery* in Trafalgar Square. It has many famous paintings. You can see paintings by Turner, Constable, Goya, Van Dyck, Leonardo da Vinci, Michelangelo, Rembrandt, Renoir, Rubens and Titian.

Another well-known London gallery is *The Tate Gallery*, on the north bank of the river Thames. It was built in 1897.

The Tate Modern is a new gallery: it opened in 2000. It has a lot of modern art collections by artists like Picasso and Andy Warhol.

An Egyptian artefact at the British Museum

Museums

London has many interesting museums. *The British Museum* is one of the largest museums in the world. There are thousands of exhibits and over five kilometres of galleries. The museum has regular special exhibitions, for example, ancient Roman and Greek art, the Egyptians and the Anglo-Saxons.

Another interesting museum is the *Victoria and Albert*. It has got the world's largest dress collection. It exhibits objects as well as paintings. These objects include: furniture, carpets, ceramics, sculpture and jewellery.

Palaces

Buckingham Palace is the London home of the Queen. You can walk from Westminster Abbey to the Palace. It is a pleasant walk through *St James's Park*.

Soldiers always guard the palace. At half past eleven every morning, you can watch the soldiers change guard. *The Queen's Gallery* is in Buckingham Palace. You can visit the gallery and see the Queen's collection of paintings.

Another of the Queen's homes is *Windsor Castle*. Windsor is near the River Thames, about forty kilometres from London. The castle is eight hundred years old.

Buckingham Palace

Parks

London is well known for its parks. There are more than eighty of them! The most famous parks, near central London, are *Hyde Park, Regent's Park* and *St James's Park*. They are all royal parks.

Hyde Park is a large park of three hundred and forty acres. In the sixteenth century, King Henry VIII hunted wild animals there! Today people relax on the grass and skate and cycle on the paths.

The Serpentine is a lake in the middle of Hyde Park. In the summer, you can go on a boat or swim there.

A music concert in a London park

Speakers' Corner is also in Hyde Park, near Marble Arch. Anyone can make a speech there.

Regent's Park is very beautiful. It is home to the *London Zoo*. There are more than six thousand animals and birds in the zoo. There is an open-air theatre in Regent's Park. You can watch Shakespeare's plays there in summer.

A lot of big, outdoor concerts are held in London's parks. Other parks to visit are *Hampstead Heath* in North London and *Clapham Common* in South London.

3
Travelling in London

The tube is London's underground railway. Its train lines can take you all over the city.

Some of the lines are very old. The Metropolitan Line opened in 1863. It is the oldest in the world. The Piccadilly Line runs from Heathrow – London's largest airport – to the centre of London.

London's underground railway – the tube

You can see much more of London from a bus. There are special open-top bus tours for tourists. They show you the sights of the city. The bus tours include river cruises and walking tours.

The tourist buses leave from Green Park, Victoria station and Marble Arch.

Passengers on an open-top bus

The Docklands Light Railway (DLR) is a modern railway line. Its trains don't have drivers! The DLR is a good way to see the Docklands and East London.

There are a lot of taxis in London. The drivers are usually friendly and helpful. You should only use black cabs or licensed taxis. The roads are very busy in Central London. There is a *Congestion Charge* for every car in central London on weekdays. You can pay your Congestion Charge online or in shops.

The buses and tube get very busy in the morning between eight o' clock and ten o'clock. They are also busy in the evening between five o' clock and half past six. It is better not to travel at these times.

You will find information centres and websites in Chapter 6 to help you travel around London.

4
Shopping

London is world famous for its shopping. *Oxford Street* is London's main shopping centre. *Selfridges* is a well-known department store on Oxford Street. The most famous shop in London is *Harrods*. It is in Knightsbridge. You can buy anything you want in Harrods!

Harrods at night

There are a lot of shops in *Covent Garden*. In the 1600's, Covent Garden was a fruit and flower market. Now you can buy clothes and antiques there. You can visit the cafes and bars. Covent Garden is famous for its street performers. You can see circus performances, singing and theatre on the street!

Soho is in central London. It is a good place to buy music. People go to *Bond Street* and *Marylebone High Street* to buy clothes and furniture.

Street performers in Covent Garden

There are also hundreds of markets in London. They sell all kinds of things: food, clothes, jewellery, music and furniture. The two best known markets are *Portobello Road* and *Camden*. Portobello Road is in West London, in Notting Hill. You can go there by tube. The nearest stations are Notting Hill Gate and Ladbroke Grove. The market sells exciting things. You can buy old clothes and antiques there. It is very popular on a Saturday.

Camden Market is in North London. It is famous for art and music. Many young people go to Camden Market. Other popular markets in London are *Spitalfields*, *Greenwich* and *Petticoat Lane*.

Camden Market

5

London at Night

Pubs, Bars and Clubs

There are more than seven thousand public houses in London! Public houses – or pubs – are usually open all day and all evening. You can eat and drink in pubs. In some pubs you can hear live music.

Outside the pubs in the West End

There are a lot of famous, old pubs in London. *The Prospect of Whitby*, in East London, is a very old pub. It was built in 1520. *The Lamb and Flag* in Covent Garden is more than three hundred years old. Covent Garden also has a lot of bars. They stay open much later than pubs. Bars often have dancing.

Notting Hill is a good place to visit at night. It has the largest carnival in Europe. More than a million people go there every August. They look at the colourful costumes and dance.

Notting Hill Carnival

There are many nightclubs in London. Some nightclubs stay open all night. You will find many bars and clubs in Soho. They play all kinds of different music.

You can hear live music and bands in London too. You can buy a newspaper or entertainment guide to find out what live events are happening.

A live band at *The Mean Fiddler* in London

Theatres and Cinemas

Most theatres and cinemas in London are in the *West End*. The nearest tube stations are Piccadilly Circus and Leicester Square. You can see all kinds of plays and shows in London's theatres. There are musicals, comedies and plays by modern writers.

West End theatres at night

The National Theatre and the *Barbican Centre* are good places to see plays.

You can also go to the Globe Theatre, by the River Thames. It is a modern theatre but it looks like Shakespeare's Globe. You can see a picture of the new Globe on page 7. You can also see Shakespeare's plays at the open-air theatre in Regent's Park.

You can see first showings of new films in West End cinemas. There are also a lot of small cinemas all over London. They show interesting, low-budget films.

Restaurants

In Soho there are many foreign restaurants and cafés. You can go for an expensive meal there, or you can eat very cheaply. There are a lot of good Chinese restaurants on Gerrard Street in Soho. The area is known as *Chinatown*.

Chinatown

You can eat food from all over the world in London. You can go to French, Italian, Spanish, Caribbean, Thai, Greek, Turkish, Indian, Japanese, African or Chinese restaurants. Some of the most famous restaurants in the world are in London.

6

Information and Advice

Perhaps you will visit London one day. Here is some advice:

- Buy a good map.
- Check the internet to find out what is on.
- Remember to ask for help – people can be friendly.
- London is a great city – have fun!

Tourist Offices

The British Visitor Centre
1 Lower Regent Street (near Piccadilly Circus)

There is also the London Visitor Centre in Arrivals at Waterloo International Station. **www.visitbritain.com**

The London Tourist Board
Go to **www.londontouristboard.com**

Travel Information

Transport for London (TfL) travel information offices are at:
Piccadilly Circus, Euston, Liverpool Street, Paddington and Victoria train stations, Victoria Coach Station, and Heathrow, Terminals one, two and three, West Croydon Bus Station and Camden Town Hall.

Twenty-four hour phone line: 020 7222 1234
Website: **www.tfl.gov.uk**

Useful websites

www.londontown.com This is a website for first-time visitors to London. It has information on hotels, sights and restaurants.

www.24hourmuseum.co.uk This is a website with information on every single museum in London.

Here are some good websites with information on hotels, theatres, cinemas, pubs and bars:
www.londonnet.co.uk
www.viewlondon.co.uk
www.timeout.com/london

Here are some websites to help you find an address and plan your route:
www.streetmap.co.uk
www.multimap.co.uk

Useful telephone numbers

Emergency – police, fire or ambulance: national emergency 999

Directory enquiries: 118 500 or 118 118

Exercises

Prepositions: *in at on*

Put the correct preposition in the following sentences:

1 London is the biggest city .... Britain.

2 There are lots of places to go .... night.

3 The Romans built a town .... the River Thames.

4 Shakespeare was born .... Stratford-on-Avon.

5 Charles Dickens lived .... Doughty Street.

6 You can ride all over the city .... the tube.

7 The Metropolitan is the oldest underground line .... the world.

8 You can get .... a river boat .... Westminster Bridge.

Jumbled sentences: put the words in the correct order

These are sentences from the book. Can you put the words in the correct order?

Example	the north of old buildings are Most famous of the river.
You write:	*Most of the famous old buildings are north of the river.*

1	the great British museums is one of The Museum of the world.
You write:	
2	You can go by visiting inside Buckingham Palace the Queen's Gallery.
You write:	
3	The Hyde Park is Serpentine in the middle of a lake.
You write:	

36

What can you do? Where?

Use the words and phrases in the boxes. Make sentences like the example:

see	modern plays and musicals	all over	Soho restaurants
watch	ancient Roman and Greek art	at	Greenwich
visit	the Old Royal Observatory	in	the city
take	many different kinds of food	in	West End theatres
eat	the tube	at	the British Museum

Example *You can visit the Old Royal Observatory in Greenwich.*

1 _____

2 _____

3 _____

4 _____

A good place to go: questions and answers

Make questions for these answers. The first one is an example:

You write **When** *is the best time to visit Notting Hill?*
Example The best time to visit Notting Hill is at night.

1 **Where** ?

Charles Dickens lived in Doughty Street.

2 **When** ?

The Great Fire of London started in September 1666.

3 **How** ?

Westminster Abbey is more than nine hundred years old.

4 **How** ?

The London Eye is 135 metres high.

5 **What** ?

Big Ben is the name of a bell and also the name of a clock tower.

Locations: places on a map

Here are some of the underground stations and places in central London.

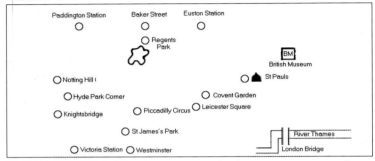

Can you work out these place names? The first one is an example.

Anagram	Place Name	Information
LONG DONE BIRD	*London Bridge*	This was the first bridge to cross the river Thames.
LAST SUP		You can see this cathedral from the *London Eye*.
MUST BRUISE HIM		You can see old Greek and Roman art here.
QUEST SEALER ICER		Many theatres and cinemas are near here.
STARK PENGER		London Zoo and an open-air theatre are in this place.
MINT STEWERS		The Houses of Parliament and Big Ben are here – and a famous abbey.
AVIRICOT		This is the name of a famous Queen of England.
TEND RAVEN COG		The Royal Opera House is here, and many bars and outdoor cafes.

OLL NIGHT TIN		This is the site of an annual carnival.

Complete the story: fill in the gaps

Use the words in the box to complete the story.

> homeless   died   old   in   cleaner   rubbish   bad
> people   bakery   city   houses   and   started   fire   of
> the   a   understand   ate   Thames   days   destroyed
> called   It

The Plague and the Great Fire of London

The population of London [1]............... 1665 was about 250,000
[2]............... . It was the largest [3]............... in Europe. But the
[4]............... were very close together, [5]............... the houses were
made [6]............... wood. There were many fires in [7]............... old
city.

London was [8]............... dirty city. People threw [9]............... into
the streets. Dogs and rats [10]............... the rubbish. The River
[11]............... was an open sewer. It smelt [12]............... . Sickness
spread quickly. In 1665 people [13]............... to die from a disease
[14]............... the *bubonic plague*. Thousands of people
[15]...............from this disease. Doctors did not [16]............... how the
disease spread.

There was a great [17]...............in the following year. The Great Fire of
London started in a [18]............... It lasted for five [19]...............,
from 2nd September 1666. [20] .... destroyed almost all of the
[21]............... city. Over 13,000 houses were [22]............... . Over
100,000 people became [23]..............., but very few people died in the
fire.

After the fire, London was a [24]............... place – for a short time.

Macmillan Education
The Macmillan Building
4 Crinan Street
London N1 9XW
A division of Macmillan Publishers Limited
Companies and representatives throughout the world

ISBN 978-0-230-03509-6
ISBN 978-1-4050-8711-7 (with CD pack)

First published 2006
Text © Philip Prowse 2006
Design and illustration © Macmillan Publishers Limited 2006

This version first published 2006

All rights reserved; no part of this publication may be
reproduced, stored in a retrieval system, transmitted in any
form, or by any means, electronic, mechanical, photocopying,
recording, or otherwise, without the prior written permission of
the publishers.

Cover photo by Getty Images

The authors and publishers would like to thank the following for
permission to reproduce photographs their photographic material:
Art Directors and Trip pp7, 22, 25, 26, 27, 28, 29; Corbis / Historical
Picture Archive p8, Corbis / Stapleton Collection p9; Eye Ubiquitous pp4,
12, 13, 16, 18; Getty Images pp6, 10, 11, 17, 19, 20, 23, 31, 32; Lonely
Planet p14/15; (c)Peter Froste at the Museum of London p5; Redferns p30.

Printed and bound in Thailand
2013   2012   2011
7   6   5   4

with CD pack
2015   2014   2013
15   14   13   12